Little Stars

Little Stars GOLF

Taylor Farley

A Crabtree Seedlings Book

Crabtree Publishing
crabtreebooks.com

Let's go to the **golf course**!

We will need golf clubs and golf balls.

golf clubs

tee

I will **tee off** first.

I stand with my feet apart.

I use both hands and swing my club high.

R11

I hit the ball hard onto the **fairway**.

R11

We ride a golf cart to the fairway.

I get my ball to the **putting green** in four **strokes**.

My ball is close to the hole.

I **putt** the ball softly—
it goes in!

Glossary

fairway (FAIR-way): The fairway is the short grass between the tee boxes and the putting green.

golf course (GOLF KORSS): A golf course is the grounds where golf is played. A golf course has 9 or 18 holes.

putt (PUHT): A putt is a stroke made by tapping the ball, not hitting it hard.

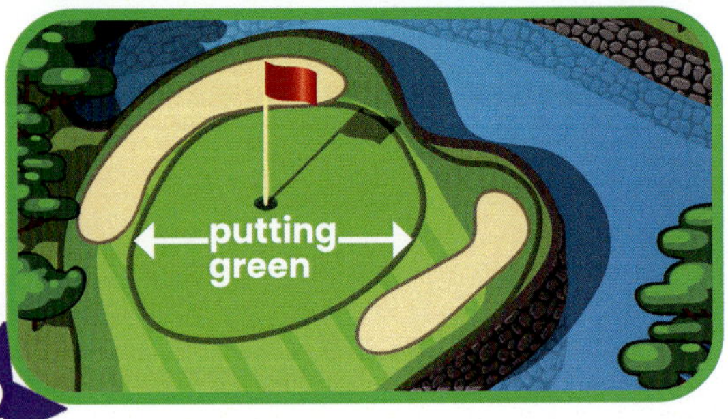

putting green (PUHT-ing GREEN): A putting green is the area around a hole.

strokes (STROKES): Strokes are any hits, or strikes, of the golf ball.

tee off (TEE OFF): To tee off is to start play by hitting a golf ball from the tee.

Index

School-to-Home Support for Caregivers and Teachers

Crabtree Seedlings books help children grow by letting them practice reading. Here are a few guiding questions to help the reader build his or her comprehension skills. Possible answers are included.

Before Reading

- **What do I think this book is about?** I think this book is about playing golf. It might tell us how children learn to play golf.
- **What do I want to learn about this topic?** I want to learn how golfers hit the ball.

During Reading

- **I wonder why...** I wonder why the golfer stands with his feet apart.
- **What have I learned so far?** I learned that a golfer uses both hands and swings a club high to hit the ball.

After Reading

- **What details did I learn about this topic?** I learned that a golf course has different parts, such as a fairway, a putting green, and a hole.
- **Write down unfamiliar words and ask questions to help understand their meaning.** I see the word *strokes* on page 17 and the word *putt* on page 20. The other vocabulary words are listed on pages 22 and 23.

Crabtree Publishing

crabtreebooks.com 800-387-7650

 In Canada: We acknowledge the financial support of the Government of Canada through the Canada Book Fund for our publishing activities.

Hardcover 978-1-4271-2978-9
Paperback 978-1-4271-2996-3

Printed in Canada/092023/
CPC20230928

Published in Canada
Crabtree Publishing
616 Welland Avenue
St. Catharines, Ontario
L2M 5V6

Published in the United States
Crabtree Publishing
347 Fifth Avenue
Suite 1402-145
New York, NY 10016

Written by: Taylor Farley
Print book version produced jointly with Blue Door Education in 2023

Photo Credits: Cover © Olimpik; page 3 © sunday hill; page 5 © SARAPON; page 6 © KK Tan; page 8, 11 and 13 © Phil's Mommy; page 14 and 16 © Dasha Petrenko; page 19 © Mr.Somchai Sukkasem; page 21 © Click Images; page 22 and 23 top photos © i am way, page 22 bottom © Lapina; page 23 middle © Olimpik All images from Shutterstock.com

Library and Archives Canada Cataloguing in Publication
Available at the Library and Archives Canada

Library of Congress Cataloging-in-Publication Data
Available at the Library of Congress